LIKE A COAT OF MANY COLORS

EDITH COVENSKY WRITES SYMBOLIST POETRY

LIKE A COAT OF MANY COLORS

EDITH COVENSKY WRITES SYMBOLIST POETRY

YAIR MAZOR

HenschelHAUS Publishing, Inc.
Milwaukee, Wisconsin

Published by
HenschelHAUS Publishing, Inc.
www.henschelHAUSbooks.com

ISBN: 978159598-935-2
E-ISBN:978159598-936-9
LCCN: 2022950716

For Yaara, Yaara Ben David,
a stupendous poetess, a gifted artist,
a remarkable singer,
and a true, devoted friend,
whose prudent advice is as precious as gold.

"We are coming...into the region where we balance probabilities and choose the most likely."
—Sherlock Holmes

"The world is full of obvious things which nobody at any chance ever observes."
—Sherlock Holmes

CONTENTS

PREFACE

The definitive manifest of symbolism was published in September 1886 in an article in *Le Figaro* by Jean Moréas. He claims that naturalism and romanticism in poetry should be things of the past, and symbolist poetry should take their place. Moréas founded the symbolist movement in poetry, which the prominent poets Rimbaud, Verlaine, Malarmé, and Baudelaire predicted because they saw in the symbolist poetry an artistic medium that would influence the senses, the feelings, and the imagination of the reader. They emphasized especially the musical component in the symbolist poetry because there is nothing like music to influence the feelings of the target audience. This important principle in the symbolist poetry was in Baudelaire's poem "Les Correspondences" and in the book of symbolist poetry *The Flowers of Evil*, or *Les Fleurs du Mal* (1857).

The symbolism in poetry was influenced to a large extent by decadent literature. The symbolists emphasized evocation of the moods. They hoped to create magical power of words and the mythical nature of words. In the poem "Les Correspondences" a sensation is created of a man wandering in a forest of symbols. The symbolists saw the poem as a mystery that the reader has to decipher. In "Les Correspondences," the entire universe has meaning and feelings of sight, sound, taste, smell, and dreaming.

Provoking the laws of reality and building an alternative, imaginative, symbolic reality which dismantles the traditional connections between different elements, symbolist poetry places a new system of connections that challenge the connections in reality. The traditional reality is exchanged with the dreamlike reality, which is riddle-like and does not address rationalism, but rather focuses on emotionalism. The symbolist poem takes the reader to a world of perfect beauty, a spiritual world of celestial life where "nature is like a temple" (Baudelaire). The symbolist poem detaches reader from their daily reality; "time disappears, eternity rules—an eternity of pleasures" (Baudelaire). The symbolist poem creates a hermetic, divine world that only elevated individuals can enter. The symbolist poem creates a "pure" piece (Mallarmé) like those peacocks in the poem of Maurice Maeterlinck.

For readers to experience this well-wrought beauty is the main goal of the symbolist poem.

The poem is supposed to affect the reader as music, alcohol, or an intoxicating scent; it should hypnotize him/her, detach him/her from concrete reality, mute his/her rational judgment, and enable him/her to totally surrender to the pure pleasure of the senses.

The "tangible" reality, which is seemingly described in the symbolist poem, stimulates a mysterious, mystic, opaque, dreamlike impression. The blurring of the imagery in the picture of the poem contributes to the dreamlike characteristics of the symbolist poem; it is not clear what exactly is happening and when, and there is no ability to connect the details of the picture to any event that has happened in the past or the present. The symbolist poem creates a feeling of clouding the senses, of hallucination. The symbolist poem combines experiences that are conflicting each other in the concrete reality. The symbolist poem enlists rare words that express the desire to combine the concrete and abstract. The symbolist poem displays such a metaphorical and compressed burden on the reader, that it is hard for him/her to decipher the poem.

INTRODUCTION:

THE LITERARY MOVEMENT IN THE SYMBOLIST POETRY OF EDITH COVENSKY

This introductory chapter does not pretend to include and to map all the poetic traits of the symbolist poetry, but rather to briefly point out the characteristics of the symbolist poems and their images in a limited selection of the poetry of Edith Covensky. This symbolist manifesto challenges the realistic, naturalistic, and romantic movements in poetry, which holds the earth to reality. The symbolist poems offer alternative reality, which is based on sensual imagination, feelings, and opaque dreamlike reality. The leading, prominent poets in the symbolist movement were Baudelaire, Rimbaud, Verlaine, and Mallarmé.

The most prominent poem in this book is "Les Correspondences," which is similar to a forest of symbols in which the reader is walking and is asked to decipher the cryptic, latent meaning of the poem. If the symbolist poetry seems opaque, it is because symbolist poetry was influenced quite a bit by the decadence literature. The symbolism focuses on the magical power of the words and the mysterious character of the words. The symbolism requests readers to produce an opaque fusion of feelings, of sight, of sound, of taste, of color, of a dream.

(The following poems are all written by Edith Covensky.)

I Invent the Sun

I am caught up in the signs of the day
Enchanted, seduced in the flow
Between objects and symbols
Smudging the rules of the poem.

I hoard the breadth of words
Invent the sun
As if grasping the celestial bodies
Hovering above all this.

Ever since I pierce my sadness
Archetypical sea
Gnawing away in the sand
Construct my poems daily
To conquer the dark.

An Illusory Day

My day is illusory
Restores love perfected in me
Saved in the archives in which I focus all the sun.

And I walk solitary
A silhouette among the landscape shards
Nourishing the poem.

And still I scatter my fear with fluent rhythm
And exact rhyme
Created from the water.

An Air

My time is wind
Roaming among words contradicting one another
Glistening in the bustle of a day
And a primeval illusion
And a dark sun floats to the water's edge
And night plays
In blue language exiled from bank to bank
Like a note flowing on the page
Covered by music
With love extended in jest
Growing in the harvest of my dream
Poured out in summer longing
And a color of gleaming earth
And light enfolded insistent on being a poem.

The symbolist poem challenges the daily reality and provokes it, offering its own version of reality, like in the symbolist painting of Mark Chagall, in which the familiar reality is denied, and in its place, lie fictional laws. For example, a fish with wings stands on a large wall clock; a groom and a bride fly in the air; a big chicken is the size of the Eiffel Tower next to which it stands; a couple wearing blue dances in the air; a huge blue cow watches Paris. The elements within the paintings are replaced with unrealistic elements. The reality in the symbolist poetry deviates from the earthly, normal reality and offers a reality that is totally the opposite—a reality that is dreamy or mysterious. Baudelaire claimed that the symbolist poem takes the reader to a world of complete beauty—a spiritual world where nature is like a temple.

A Ballad

I am born from the poem's breath
Looking for identity in sound filled things
Revealing myself
Twisted in a kind of delusion.

And the sea silences my voice
Playing with still words
Revolving across the puzzle of night
Folding up amid the gusts of wind
And the illusion of my lips
In a sea of signs flowing in such absurdity.

I insist on existing between a living day
and its collapse.

For Novalis

My pain is akin to the night
Flowing in blue time
Roaming among shadows
Square on the page.

And I bend a flower
With warm desire
Create a poem
And a sandpiper bursts through a middle of such a day.

And the speech is revealed
Selective
Full of beauty
And clear music within me
Visible in this invention.

Identities

I annul time
Standing across the night
In a cluster of enchanting love
Rolling in a girl's chat pointing to the whole sky.

My day is still
Flows with my longings in a childish plot
Curling on the sand
Moving from identity to identity.

And I sing with the wind
Circle the length and breadth
Between adorning stars
Drawn in blue pencil.

The symbolist poem disconnects the reader from daily, true reality. As Baudelaire writes, "Time disappeared; eternity rules—the eternity of pleasures." The symbolist poem requests to create a "pure" piece (Mallarme), amazing in its beauty, like those peacocks in the poem by Maurice Maeterlinck, "Despair." The experience of the distilled beauty is the main goal of the symbolist poet. The symbolist poem asks to create an exalted, hermetic world that only elevated individuals can enter.

New Words Ring Strange to Me

New words ring strange to me
And my day turns to dusk
In the shade of a great hour.

And in my fictitious nest
Drive the light from the dark
Scissor a book from the contradictions.

How do I find a flower
And how concealed
In laughter
Do I investigate stars

Cleaving the clamor of day
Musing out of loneliness
And my eyes are mortal.

Black Rain

My silence is night
Facing a star flowing in a stain of light
Moving on the map of time
Like pure yearning of God.

And the bird kneels
In confession wilting in the wind
And in the flow of day renewed in the instant's sanity
Surviving at the light of the sea.

And the rain is black
Across a tear dropping on a stone
In endless stammer
And remnants of words cascading on the page.

And then truce is born of water
In an invention of a hardened poem
And use of a lofty dream
And the tune's roar making music from inside.

I Am Creating a Flower

I am creating a flower
And a woman and man:
Descendants of sun

And I fold a medium fig leaf
And a petal
In the fingertips of my love.

And a tree reaches the wall of the house
In the zone of my childhood, in human dimensions
Pierced in ancient Braille.

And I write words on scraps of paper
And on the edges of last sidewalks
And on hands that catch in
The brittle air

And my writing content
Mingles with Bartok's Suite
1923.

The symbolist poem acts on the reader like music, like alcohol or intoxicating scents, to hypnotize the reader, detach him/her from the earthly reality, to mute his/her rational thought, and to completely addict him to the total pleasure of the senses. The dreamy characteristics of the symbolist poem contribute to the blurring of the identity of the details of the picture. It's not clear what is exactly happening and when, and there is no ability to connect those details to any event that has happened in the past or present.

The symbolist poem creates a feeling of clouding the senses and delirium. The symbolist poem merges experiences that are contradictory to each other in earthly reality, such as experiences that are considered low and insignificant in the earthly reality with experiences that are considered exalted in the earthly reality. The symbolist poem enlists rare words that express an aspiration to merge the concrete and abstract. The symbolist poem demonstrates a metaphoric burden, full and compressed, which is hard for the reader to decipher.

Absurdity

My day is hushed
Revolving in the current
Twisting in the circle of water
Moving in the beauty of change
With a kind of absurd joy
Rising in the mouth of the poet.

And I whisper words among the shreds of wind
Curling in the wave of light
Hewn across the nothingness of the night
Knowing a poem
Diluted among all the fancies.

I Break the Silence

I break the silence
Enfolded among bright stars
Crowding at the edge of night
Flowing in a paradox of great light.

And my longings curl
Like a sea bird
Drawn with the myth of legend
Absurd is pining.

And the fantasy is composed from the stuff of water
And from the reelings of wind
And from the chill of the poem
In an instant creating all the words.

For Prometheus

I have plenty of things near the poem
Indicating words according to the night
Living like Prometheus
Stealing fire
Trapping love in an instant dream
Singing with the flute against the wind
Enfolding between the lines
Crowded with pure language
Amid the stains of evil laughter
Hoarding time falling into water
In a landscape flowing to the formless dark
Rolling in a dizzying drawing
Closing on my memory.

It is possible maybe to compare a symbolist poem to an ancient literary text like the Akkadian text, which was written in cuneiform script, or an ancient Egyptian text, which was written in hieroglyphic script. When we talk about symbolist poetry, each and every poem has a hidden alphabet of its own, and there is a need to decode this cryptic symbolist alphabet in order to decipher the riddle of the poem and to understand its meaning. The following chapter deals with interpretive challenges that are pre-sented by ten symbolist poems by Edith Covensky.

My Mother Perceived as Fiction

My mother perceived as fiction
Her walk fetching
Her body composed of my pranks

And she is energetic and daring
Her windings staying beyond reality.

Her place is sublime
The wrinkles on her face separate and combine
Her dress is blue
Her motion: a flower
Enclosing all summer.

Sunbeams

My poem is made like a grid
Absorbing your possible love
And the light it emits
At this hour.

My eyes stare in darkness
Whispering among the stars
Lyrical on my own terms.

And the poem reveals your face
Radiant, reviving your memory
Celebrating in my invention.

An Aberrant Night

My night is aberrant from human dimensions
Astounding river
Sensational among the verses of the poem
Divided like all contradictions
Across darkness appeased in the conflict of the moment.

And I write with much exaggeration
And with greatest music
Contained in the millions of words
Full abundant in me
Marked in the field of God.

And my love is exciting tied within me
Bursting my bounds with the enthused dynamics
In endless time
And in solitary high dialogue
Specific like sacred longing
Caught in the page's center.

The theoretical diagnoses of the symbolist poetry are drawn from Hamutal Bar-Yosef's book [in Hebrew] *Symbolism in the Modern Poetry* (published by Hakibutz Hameuchad Tel-Aviv, N.D.).

AUTHOR'S COMMENT

Like in every symbolist poem, we can describe the poetry of Edith Covensky with adjectives like mysterious, mystical, hallucinatory, dreamy, unclear, and more. Nonetheless, when I chose to do an analysis of symbolist poems by Edith Covensky, I preferred to analyze poems in which underneath the top symbolist layer, you can identify the deep artery that demonstrates traits of a causal, concrete plot. In this manner, the upper, unclear, imaginary symbolist layer has a prolific dialogue with the deep, epic layer.

INTERPRETATIONS OF SELECTED SYMBOLIST POEMS BY EDITH COVENSKY

New Words Ring Strange to Me

New words ring strange to me
And my days turn to dusk
In the shade of a great hour

And I in my fictitious nest
Drive the light from the dark
Scissor a book from disparities

How do I find a flower
And how concealed
In laughter
Do I investigate stars

Cleaving the clamor of day
Musing out of loneliness
Out of delight
And my eyes are mortal.

Reading of "New Words Ring Strange to Me"

The opening of the poem reports on and testifies to faulty communication. The new words sound strange to the ear of the speaker; consequently, the desirable communication is faulty, which is customary in symbolist poetry. The text produces several paradoxes. The speaker's day turns to dusk; nonetheless, there is an advantage in the dusk, which creates obscurity of a great hour.

Another paradox occurs when the serenity of the speaker is not real, natural, or tranquil, but rather, it is artificial; what is considered negative turns to be a positive when the speaker moves the light from the darkness.

One more paradox occurs when instead of creating a bridge between opposites, the speaker cuts a book from the opposites. Destructiveness: instead of writing a book, the speaker cuts and destroys the book. From the negativity sprouts positivity; the speaker finds a flower, and under the cover of laughter, she investigates the stars. The stars are shiny and radiant through the darkness and despair.

Here is the unity of the contradictions: while the speaker challenges the tumult of the day, she is playing out of loneliness, and the loneliness doesn't remain for a long time. The speaker does not play only out of loneliness, but also out of joy, while her eyes are human. In this way, the poem weaves a dense sequence of contradictions and paradoxes, and from that, it exhibits accordance with symbolist poetry.

I Embody the Poem

"There is a flame in creation as before sunrise."
(Uri Zvi Greenberg)

My splintered love yearns for the night
Inspires sorrow
On small paper benches

My death no longer matters

I embody the poem
Feel it not just in my head
But in my mouth too:
Words have such power.

Reading of "I Embody the Poem"

The love of the speaker is fragile and subtle. While she is fascinating herself to the night, she creates an atmosphere of sadness about everything, including innocent children's creations of small paper benches or paper sailboats that float on the lake. The death of the speaker is meaningless, unlike the dark universe, which is meaningful. What is left of the speaker is only the poem, which she experiences and feels in her entire body. This way, the words acquire tremendous power that competes with the power of the darkness of the entire universe.

The poem opens with an elegiac tone about the fragile and delicate love of the speaker, which yearns for the night and creates an atmosphere of sadness. It is like a nightly lamentation that is created. The speaker feels lost and has no energy for life, to the point where she feels that her death is not meaningful; however, the closing of the poem completely changes the lonely lamentation. Here, the poem appears and gives new life to the speaker. Indeed, the words have power like this, and above all, the sad, gothic atmosphere that opens the poem goes through a transformation and is translated into great optimism with the power of the words.

Night Falls on Narrow Streets

Night falls on narrow streets
And the moon crumbles the day
And intensifies gloom

And preserves the contrast
Between day and night
And preserves time

I save from all these
A trampled leaf falling
On the pages of the book

And a trampled dry flower
And a thin wing of a butterfly
And a wing of a plane.

Reading of "Night Falls on Narrow Streets"

The poem opens with a paradox: the moon, which is a source of light, crumbles the day and makes the darkness deeper. Indeed, the poem preserves the difference between the day and night. The poem preserves the time by prolonging the light of day and depriving the darkness of the night. Here the speaker invades the world of the poem—from the daylight, from the darkness, from the moon, from the day, from the time. She preserves a trampled leaf that fell on the paper of the book. Like this, the moon keeps the light and the time. In other words, the analogy ties together like strong glue all the different elements of the poem.

The speaker continues to commemorate everything that was—the trampled dry flower, a butterfly wing. The memory of this would have faded and disappeared without the memory of the speaker. This way, the flowing of time is challenged, and we do not let things pass without having a witness to testify to its existence in the past. In this way, even the wing of the airplane when it hovers, fades away and leaves nothing behind. In a paradoxical manner, the trampled dry flower, the trampled falling leaf, and the thin butterfly wing are stronger than the wing of the passing airplane. In contradiction to the passing airplane wing, they leave behind them traces, memory, and testimony that they existed. The poem of the speaker reinforces the memory of all of these with the word, with syntax, with the color of the sound.

Still Life

A table stands here
There a window opens to the air
The light pierces the recesses of my body

And in a trance
A woman's face becomes an icon
Canceling the night

How splendid her words
How lonely
Her attire the silk of a princess
Her smile undrawn.

Reading of "Still Life"

Apparently, the reality is earthly, but in fact, there is something mysterious, mystical, dream-like, which demonstrates the elements of fantasy. Is it possible to interpret differently the light, which penetrates the internal parts of the speaker's body? Is this a state of dreaming when the face of the woman turns into a portrait and cancels the night? The third and last stanza focuses on the speaker by herself. Like her portrait radiates light, in the same way, her words shine. Even here, the reality denies the rules of earthly reality. Nonetheless, in spite of the brightness that shines, the loneliness connected to the brightness of the speaker's speech (hallucinatory metaphor and not an earthly metaphor), and the loneliness of her attire made out of the silk of princesses, the beauty which conquers the heart is mixed with a burning sadness.

"Her smile undrawn" acts like the entire poem—in the twilight zone, which is between the dreamy hallucination and the earthly reality. If her smile, like the smile of the Mona Lisa, is not drawn, what will it look like; it is a paradox! Like in the symbolist poetry, it is not clear where the hallucinated reality of the fantasy is happening. The contradictions are bound to each other, and the pictures are silent and frozen, in contradiction to the dynamics that characterize romantic poetry.

Blessings

As on wine my blessing is on love
Believing with ease that beauty saves
And that the sun is like a window
Above the height of the eyes.

I have traded smiles with a boy in the street
Indicating playfully
A birth certificate
And identity card
In a chronicle of nowhere else.

My body was frozen in dance
Yours has beguiled me to forget
Whirled me into his own reality
Approaching the close.

Reading of "Blessings"

The speaker blesses her love, like blessing over the wine before the evening of the Sabbath in a Jewish ritual. In this way, the blessing of her love is given a holy, mystical dimension. She is full of optimism and joy of life. She easily believes that the beauty influences while the fluent light of the sun permeates and penetrates all the corners of the room, like through a window above the height of the eyes. The happiness and lightness that the speaker feels while she is soaked with the light of the sun bring her to conduct an amusing dialogue with a child in the street.

The third stanza, surprisingly, denies and ignores the warmth, the light, and the amusement that are expressed in the first two stanzas. The body of the speaker is frozen in dance. Only the body of the male recipient causes the speaker to forget, while at the same time, takes her to the vital reality of his life.

All of this is close to the closing of the poem, like the closing prayer at the end of Yom Kippur. The poem, which opens in a religious prayer, finds its end in a religious prayer and atones for all the sins. The transition in the poem, from one extreme full of optimism and effervescence which comes from the joy of life and where we bless love like the blessing over wine, to the other, blatant extreme where the frozen body of the speaker produces a paradox. The unity of the contradictions is typical of the characteristics of symbolist poetry.

Alias

My name is made up
A kind of imaginary biography
Resolutely twisted

Like a picturesque model
Too serious to be synthetic
Shattering regular habits of sight
In a game of identities
And exchanges of time
And exchanges of place.

I cannot explain these signs
Finally I am marginal in my writing
With a name complex
And old time

Erupting in the storm of words
On a public bench
And writing again on the sand
What the sea will not erase.

Reading of "Alias"

The speaker testifies about herself that she is a prisoner in the maze of lies; her name is made up, and her biography is hallucinated and twisted. She visualizes her hallucinated biography like a drawing: serious, authentic, smashing all the basic habits of sight; and she denies any showing of common sense. There is confusion in the game of exchanging identities, time, and place, and every possibility of logical attachment is disrupted and condemned in advance to failure. Every stable orientation collapses and shatters.

The speaker testifies about herself that she fails in her ability to decipher and interpret all these signs, and therefore, she stays insignificant in her writing without the leading and directing hand of the speaker. Because the speaker herself loses the ability to lead, she is dropped from the path of writing. She stays behind, unable to control the storm of the words.

Her writing in the sand—"what the sea will not erase"— is a wish and an illusion at the same time. The imaginary identity, the imaginary biography, the smashing of the basic habits of sight, the game of switching identities (one after the other), the exchanging of the time and of place: all these create a stormy sense of shaking, embarrassment, a loss of direction. These are characteristics of many symbolist poems. The speaker, defeated by embarrassment, stays marginal without lacking any ability to interpret or to understand the world in which she is ensnared; all she has now is the illusion, the wish that will never come true.

Signs of Time

I contemplated your confusion
My eyes searched your depths
With burning letters on the edge of language.

I was silent
Because of the night's weight
Thought after thought
And soft weaknesses
And afterwards the cover
Of a thin rain.

I say stars
And the sun suspended on its axis
As symbols of time
The living drew me.

My busic fear stays with me as long as the sand.

Reading of "Signs of Time"

The speaker follows after the embarrassment of the male recipient. Her eyes follow him in his depth while burning letters scorch the edge of the tongue, but her searches are in vain; claims are demanded in order to execute the search and its success and not letters, not to mention, burning letters. Words and sayings attempt to provoke, challenge, attract, and persuade, but the heaviness of the night has decreed silence on the speaker, and she is pushed to the rear while thoughts haunt her. Soft weak-

nesses with a gentle rain wrap her like a veil, which wants
to wrap and comfort her. Since the time is the night hour,
the speaker sees stars, but in a paradoxical way, she sees
a sun that hangs on the side to show the specifics of time.

The specifics of time are implied at the end of the poem
while mentioning the sand, which reminds us of an
hourglass. The hourglass feeds the fear of the speaker
because it documents the time running out. Indeed, not
for vain, the living attracts her. She rebels against the time
running out, against the death, which hounds her. The
poem that opens with a pining after the male recipient—a
search that was doomed from the beginning to fail—
transfers to disheartening experiences of the speaker and
is sealed with her fear of death, which is fed by the hourglass.

Odysseus

A lover's wind plays and schemes in me
Exchanging signs of secrecy
Among the cats on a tense street.

The shape of man shocks me
Hung like a cloud
Dusty from my tryings
Begun in my wanderings.

My spirit springs up like a storm
Touching me and not touching
Fastening my lips to the night
In such aloneness.

Reading of "Odysseus"

The lover's wind that plays with the speaker's mind is deceiving her and leading her astray; it becomes clear as a plotting evil wind. This is a vicious wind that exchanges cryptic secrets in its nocturnal solitude of a street that is dismayed and anxious. Only the street cats stroll in the deserted street. The disappointment, from the conspiring, betraying, evil lover's wind, causes the speaker to lose trust in human beings, which she portrays like an evaporated, dissolving cloud. It seems like the cloud, which is blanketed with dust, is similar to the attempts of the speaker; the attempts begin with the wanderings towards the unknown future.

The disappointment is full of fear, moving like a branch in the wind, a lost spirit in the storm. Her lips attach to the night and to the loneliness, which don't give her rest. Therefore, she stays trapped in a cage of her disappointment and distress. The promise of her loved one, which is given to the speaker, shatters in a dizzying speed and abandons the speaker to her burning, scared disappointment. The reality portrayed in the poem is foreign, strange, and hallucinatory. A thorny reality in which we can locate signs and elements of fantasy is common in symbolist poetry.

Expected Love

A woman is writing a poem: creating illusions
Without exact definitions
And of no school.

Love exists in her head
And still more in her momentary silence.

The rain's chemicals no longer frighten her
Her smile is legible on her forehead
Her tongue does not fail

And what she writes lives only in the page's center.

Reading of "Expected Love"

The writing of poetry dictates creation of illusions. The same illusions are lacking precise definitions because every poem is a product of creative imagination, which is not trapped in any rules of convention. The love already exists in the head and the heart of the speaker even before she writes it. Even more than that, the love is developed and exists already in the momentary silence of the speaker.

The poet is captured in her poetry (in the positive aspect of the words). The soaked chemicals in the rain again do not frighten her, and her speech does not fail. The smile, which is engraved in her forehead, expresses the joy of her creation. What the speaker writes is imprinted only in the center of the page, not in the margins, without any fear that it will slip and drop because it is in a stable, solid place—not a secret place, but in a place that declares itself with courage.

This is an optimistic poem which amalgamates writing of poetry and love, and in both of them, strength is cast forth and is not locked, hidden, or repressed. Only joy is written here, and there is nothing that will darken it. Therefore, behind the symbolist blurring that is apparently ambiguous, a systematic, organized system of sayings which nurture a mutual relationship of expressions exists.

The Flow of the Poem

My lips run sparingly in the flow of the poem
Crossing from bank to bank
The first sobs of my life.

And I write words
Like a Japanese painter amazed by her intuition
Carrying my internal flesh in a blaze.

For some time
I have turned my attention from this page
Enfolding the break in myself
In an intoxication of sobriety.

Smirk as a poet
In a brief essay
The poem is carved from.

Reading of "The Flow of the Poem"

The poem is a confession of the speaker, which reports the process of writing her poetry. The timing of the poem is exposed after the symbolist layers are peeled. First, the poem can be described in terms of a birth. Its underdeveloped language (like the beginning language of a baby) still cannot swim along the river (the poem), but only to cross from bank to bank. This is the beginning of the birth of writing a poem.

The crying of the speaker in her first years of life is like the crying of a baby. Even here, the metaphor in which the two are combined—the birth of the poem and the birth of a child—is extended and stretched. The fact that the speaker writes words like a minimalist Japanese painter (not to mention, the Japanese Haiku poem) comes back and echoes the language of the minimalist poetry of the speaker: moderate, minimalist. Therefore, behind the reduction and the restraint of the poetry of the speaker, like a minimalist Japanese painter and a small, Japanese Haiku poem, there is an internal burning fire through the process of writing her poetry.

The speaker goes through and experiences a crisis in the process of writing her poetry; she distracts herself from the written page while she is getting addicted to the intoxication of becoming sober. Here, she is mocking the poet, who is writing a short essay from which "the poem is carved." Here is the paradox: the short essay is written about the poem, but in fact, the poem is not carved from the short essay because the writing of the poem preceded the writing of the essay. Even here, the common paradox in symbolist poetry is found, and is rooted in the foundation of the poem; this is a poem about losing the identity of the same poem itself.

To Dali

I sift through words
Where the poem exists
My borders liquid in a plain solid way.

I have tools to deceive myself
With love which gives birth to the set of my sketches
And fixes stars in their paths
Till the rain spoils my hopes.

And I dictate words in the night
Writing my silence
And my aged decrepit head
Rejects temptations
One by one.

Reading of "To Dali"

Even this poem, like many other of Edith Covensky's poems, focuses on the complex and often exhausting process of writing poetry. "I sift through words" means that the process of writing poetry is very aware of itself, polished and punctual. The boundaries of the speaker are fluid in a very simple, physical way, which means that the speaker has to put an end to the boundaries in order to engage in the process of writing the poem; here is the paradox. The speaker has tools, which are designated specifically to delude herself and to teach the reader how much she is aware of herself and her abilities. The self-delusion is translated in a surprising way to love, which produces the series of her poems, the same love that determines and dictates the series and the styles of her poetry in their path.

The speaker understands the process of the writing of the poetry as a cosmic process of creation until the earthly rain comes and breaches the cosmic feeling and disproves the expectations of the speaker. The rain negates the speaker's delusion and leaves her abandoned and disappointed.

The writing of the speaker is nocturnal in the sense that it is written in the night when she is surrounded by her silence. Her head is full of the experiences, the sensations, the feelings like an old head that rejects the temptations to less painful experiences. The rain refutes and makes angry the expectations of the speaker while she is holding onto her delusion that the process of writing poetry is a cosmic process; the same delusion collapses and shatters to the ground of the earthly reality, and the speaker wallows in her disappointment and her pain.

An Attempt to Write

My love is constant on the surface of the poem
Seeking its way in creation
Nourished by the primal matter
And the beauty that dwells between the lines.

And the poem is fictive and true
A fragile double invention
Overflowing my bounds
Composed between the words.

My night of love happens in song
Lives in my storied body
Dashed in the great experiment of my writing.

Reading of "An Attempt to Write"

(Another poem of *Ars Poetica*, one of many)

The speaker is searching her personal path in the designing of her creation, and she is nourished from the beginning of the poem. The poem is real and false at the same time, like a saying that is common in the Arabic and Hebrew poetry in the Middle Ages in Muslim Spain: "Falseness=the best of the poem." Therefore, the poem itself is fiction, which materializes as real. The delicate fragility of the poem is expressed between the words. The speaker feels the sensual merging with the poetry, until the night of love is happening in the poem, which is like in the legend; in a paradoxical way, the night turns into a realistic lie. Like the best of the traditional symbolist poetry, the poem documents the process of writing poetry. The process is cryptic and opaque—almost mystic—and only outstanding people can enter the secret realm.

I Became a Debauched Philosopher

"The nonexistent must remain more beautiful."
(Abraham Sutzkever)

The shadow of the night
Dresses in dismal beauty
And my charming sadness
And drunken laughter
Awaken love in me.

My illusion is dreamlike
Like memories of my excitement.

I became a debauched philosopher
Amidst the waves of perfume

And the deceptions
And my spirit wandering exile
And my limits: the sea.

Reading of "I Became a Debauched Philosopher"

The first stanza of the poem shows a symbolist quality in a drawing—an ecstatic situation of spiritual uplifting of the speaker—in the poem, in the same manner that the shadow of the night wears a dark beauty, sadness of the speaker. Her drunken laughter from rising feelings awakens love in her. Indeed, she is without illusions, but her dreamy illusion is like the memories of her excitement.

Philosophy is based on solid, pure logic, but the speaker challenges her own definition of philosophy; the quality of the philosophy is a philosophy of debauchery. After the spiritual uplifting comes the painful sobriety. The illusions sabotage her spirit, which is lifted up; her spirit is compared to wanderers who are exiled from the anchor. Her limit is the ocean, which covers with indifference over her stormy feelings—the same way the pride of her feelings is collapsed and destroyed on the ground of the cold reality, isolated and full of disappointment.

Toils

I touched your head
Dense in toils and weaknesses
And human delusions.

And your body is tangibly warm

(that is existent)
Dancing to sometime

There is much clarity in this silence
The water is also limpid in quietness
Connecting to the poem
From the words of your longings.

I become pensive
And my mind draws a kind of sea in yellow light
Dripping the liquid of your love.

Reading of "Toils"

The song is a typical sensual love song that the speaker
writes to her loved one, the mysterious male recipient. The
erotic love motif is supported in the poem from the spirit of
the allusions from *Songs of Songs*. The speaker, who is
touching the head of her loved one in *Song of Songs*, which
is the head full of dew, but here, the Biblical allusion to
Song of Songs is cracked; thus, the thick head of the loved
one in the poem is full of weaknesses and human illu-

sions, let alone, poked and confined to the reality of the distress. Nonetheless, the body of the loved one is very concrete and tangible, warm and perceptible.

Traces of Love

Traces of my love are suspended
Each with own language
Appearing to me in a dream

And easy wonder plays on my face
Frolics freely on the screen of my words

My attempt at love is stubborn
Ethereal in amazement
Yoked to the coach of my soul
Playful on the page

At moments my existence transpires faultlessly.

Reading of "Traces of Love"

This is another love song of the speaker-poet. The love of the speaker is like it is made out of flakes, and each one in its turn and its own special language comes to her in a dream. The reaction of the speaker is a small surprise, which plays easily on the origins of her writing. The speaker comes back and reports about her love, but this time in a different way and with a more difficult purpose. He or she testifies about her love as a stubborn attempt, as a swimmer who does not give up when attempting a challenging goal.

At the same time, the attempt shows excitement and wonder. The same love attempt—determined and stubborn—is harnessed to the wagon of her spirit, which does not give up. The speaker, despite the challenging difficulty, is full of a light spirit that is hedonistic; the speaker is almost amused while she is writing her poetry. The writing of the speaker's poetry is like a game; it causes her pleasure on the page. This demonstrated tendency leads and directs the poem to its optimistic, desired ending because the signing of the poem shows a rare moment of wholeness, of the existence of the speaker in a way that nothing can damage or reduce.

Sunbeams

My poem is made like a grid
Absorbing your possible love
And the light it emits
At this hour.

My eyes stare in darkness
Whispering among the stars
Lyrical on my own terms

And the poem reveals your face
Radiant, reviving your memory
Celebrating in my invention.

Reading of "Sunbeams"

This is an *Ars Poetica* poem, which is written in the structure of a symbolist poem. The wording is dark, strange, hallucinatory—like the words are wrapped in a mysterious, mystic blanket. The wording focuses in the internal, abstract truths: love, life, art, and poetry. The speaker compares her poetry to a crossword puzzle. The poem is imprisoning lightning; it absorbs the love of the male recipient and returns light the same way as the love projects light. The opponent of the light is documented as the darkness. Here is the paradox: from the darkness, the light breaks through.

Indeed, the eyes of the speaker are confined to the darkness, but they whisper among the stars, a fact that indicates an intimate relationship between the speaker and the stars. Indeed, like a love that projects light, so are the stars projecting light. This teaches you that the poetic eyes of the speaker are like electricity that conducts and projects the poem.

The poem opens with the male recipient of the love, just as it closes with the male recipient of the love. In many of the poems of Edith Covensky, the process of writing poetry involves love. The poem unveils the face of the male recipient, his brightness that brings back the poem to the motif of the light, and the memory of the male recipient celebrates the fictional character of the poem. Again, love and poetry intertwine with each other. Not in vain, the speaker calls her poetry a crossword puzzle. In the poem, there are different components that demonstrate reciprocal dialogues: poetry, light, memory, love.

Units of Time

Night weakens at sunrise
Curling on yellow sand
Surrendering silently.

And I muse in the midst of day
Wondering at the content of the poem
Creased by anxiety between tiny units of time

And then I consider my human condition
Discover fears reposing on my body
Dissolving in darkness.

And at a moment of high awareness
I am an engraved poem
Swaying on a damp night
Lightly decorated with magic.

Reading of "Units of Time"

The poem opens with the background of the writing of the poem; the night is deterred and pushed aside from the sprouting sunrise. In addition, the poem cuddles on the yellow sand and eventually surrenders in the silence, the quiet, and the speaker hallucinates in the middle of the day while she is wondering about the content of the written poem. She is anxious about the tiny units of time that are left for her to complete her poem.

To the speaker, the writing of the poem is bound with the strength of her existing situation. She produces fears that cling to her body while they are mixed with the darkness that encompasses her, and then, in a moment of extreme self-awareness, the poem is carved on her body while she is wet from a night that is damp. She is full of a feeling of lightness that wraps around her a feeling of pleasant magic. This way, the poem demonstrates three levels of development. The poem opens in a cosmic atmosphere, and continues with documenting the painful process of writing a poem in which fears are swarming in the darkness; the poem ends with a feeling of spiritual elevation saturated with magic, which is characteristic of symbolist poetry.

My Day Begins With Water

My day begins with water
And the salt remains in the mouth
And the sun bends the time
On the dead landscape.

They say there is beauty in this world
And there are flowers in the wind
And there is also sun
As Vivaldi writes in his music
The Seasons.

Telegraph wires connect now to every pole
And they slice through the air
And they are tall.

Reading of "My Day Begins With Water"

The opening of the poem is significantly optimistic: the speaker's day starts with water, which is a symbol of life and vitality; however, already in the following line and those that come after that, the lines deny entirely the optimism: the taste of the salt remains in the mouth; the sun challenges the time and oppresses it; and the view bound with beauty remains indifferent, exhausted, and dead.

In the second stanza, things are reversed. The first line "They say there is beauty in this world" is an allusion to a very known poetic line of Bialik ("They say there is love in this world."). Thus, like the speaker determines, there is beauty in this world, and there are flowers in the wind. There is also sun, which now does not challenge, bend, or irritate the time. Everything is so effervescent and tempestuous, like in Vivaldi's *The Seasons*; the music has a liveliness and a joy of life. In this way, the dialogue between the first stanza and the second stanza is like the thesis and antithesis.

The third stanza seals the poem, and it is like a synthesis because it contains negativity (thesis) and positivity (antithesis). On one hand, the wires of the telegraph lack vitality, but on the other hand, the telegraph wires enable human communication and human connection, which has a considerable amount of expression of life. This way, the poem positions the thesis, then the antithesis, and finally, concludes with the synthesis, which displays extreme transitions from one situation to another; these transitions give the poem a dynamic, energetic portrait.

Analysis

A few times I thought to myself:
No sign will remain of my life
Or any sign of heaven
On earth
And then I will be buried in the sea
Like a fish.

And then grass will sprout from me
And blood will rise
In the grass
And water will arise in the blood.

A war leaves signs
And a plane crossing the sky
Leaves signs

Like a bird.

Reading of "Analysis"

The opening of the poem is very pessimistic; even a frail
sign will not remain from the speaker after her death.
Even the sky and the land will not leave signs after the
fading away, and the speaker will be buried in the sea like
a fish. She will be like a rock or a stone on which seaweed
will grow. The only living thing that will remain is the
blood; on the weeds, the blood will rise, and on the blood,

the water will rise. A war that is bound not just in death, but also in wounds and scars definitely leaves signs after it. In a paradoxical way, a plane that passes in the air like a bird leaves signs after it. What can be the signs that an airplane and bird leave after them after they pass without returning? Maybe just a faint trembling, a passing breath of air that fades away quickly.

The speaker insists this: the plane and the bird that fly without coming back leave signs. Here is the paradox: there is no way to explain it rationally or to answer the question, as one can in typical symbolist poetry. All the rest will not remain and will not leave signs. Everything is destined to disappear sooner or later; everything is sentenced to die, and the pessimism of the poem does not disappear, but instead, leaves signs that will not be erased and will not be faded.

For Magritte

1929
The words are constructed on the usage of signs
Language within language
(said Rene Magritte).

Words have significance:
A black cat is not a cat
A red flower is born from the earth

A leaf can be a cannon
A cloud may be sun
Sun can be a cloud.

The words alone bind me to the tree.

Reading of "For Magritte"

Indeed, the words are symbols for certain objects, both concrete and abstract, but in the symbolist poem, the objects are in a physical state of floating, like wandering sand, which wear a shape and then change shape. A black cat (like the name of the French periodical of symbolist poetry) is not a cat, but a red flower; it is a product of the earth in the traditional meaning which obeys the laws of reality. It continues with examples of the symbolist elements, which refuse to accept the laws of traditional reality and contradict them: a leaf can be a cannon; a cloud can be a sun; a sun can be a cloud.

The words themselves tie the speaker to the tree, and for her, the words are used as an anchor. She needs the anchor in the symbolist world where the reality is not earthly, but unclear, cryptic, mysterious, and veiled. It is an *Ars Poetica* poem, in the sense that it documents a dark and confusing portrait of poetic reality in the symbolist poetry.

Poetics

The mysticism of the soul
Is sometimes a revelation of my lucidity.

My work is an abstraction
Of landscapes
And thoughts.

Ashbery repeats the formula of Horace:
Poetry is like painting.

It is easy for me to write
Easy for them to draw.

When I write now
I permit myself
The greatest freedom.

Reading of "Poetics"

[Another *Ars Poetica* poem]

In the symbolist poetry, the mysticism can produce clarity and transparency because the symbolist poetry does not obey the earthly revelation of logic. The writing of poetry produces an abstract documentation, not only of the landscapes, but also of the thoughts. Here again, there is a paradox: the thoughts are abstract by nature, and therefore, there is no need for their abstract documentation. As is common in symbolist poetry, the paradox cannot be solved, cannot be decoded, and therefore, it contributes to the mysterious atmosphere and even the mysticism of the poem.

Ashbery repeats the formula of Horace: "Poetry is like painting," which means that poetry, like painting, both are artistic representations of the earthly reality and of the emotional, spiritual reality as well. Here, it is important to bring in the diagnosis of Lessing, in his book *Laokoon*

(1766). The literature/poetry are completely different from the painting/sculpture because they are out of time (perceived through a continuum of time; whereas, the painting/sculpture are perceived through a continuum of space, and not in the continuum of time). Their emotional and concrete closeness to their medium of art makes it easier on the poet and the painter to express themselves in their chosen medium.

Therefore, when the speaker writes her poetry, her medium grants her complete freedom, freedom from all the distress of the reality. Even here, we see the tendency of symbolist poetry: total freedom from any earthly reality (historical, social, and national), and a gathering of mystic, silent, and cryptic reality—and even a reality of fantasy.

Synesis

My poem flickers at a point in time
And in a draft of specific biography
Balanced against all the days.

And my voice is primary:
A pure spark left in fantasy
Awakened under the cover of the song.

My radiant tongue brightens
Soars about me at midnight

And then love begins
Hovering silent between the arches of my window
Meshing my words in yearnings
Quaking the night.

Reading of "Synesis"

This poem is also clearly *Ars Poetica*, since it includes symbolist, aesthetic techniques. The poem is described like a rider who flickers from the distance, like in a draft of the speaker's biography. Nonetheless, the poem is equal to all the days that came before it and all the days that came after it. The voice of the poetry of the speaker has just now been created and emerged: it is pure spark that is based in fiction, and only in the territory of the poetry, it awakens for the first time.

The language of the speaker's poetry is shining, clear, and radiant, and wraps the speaker in the darkness of the night. This is the hour of love: it hovers silently between the arches of the window of the speaker. The love unites the speaker's words with the glue of longing and trembles the night with its hovering whisper. The brightness in the middle of the night to the silent love which trembles in the darkness are the center of this *ars poetica* poem. The element of fantasy, its secret and mystic portrait, and the focus on art, poetry, and love all grant the poem its symbolist characteristics.

Synesis 2

My poem mingles with a droplet of young tears
Exposes analogical sensitivities
Stamped in me since my birth.

I free myself from conventions
Touch the edges of the green
And above me are countless stars.

My thought has been defeated:
You have burst into
The chambers of my brain
And mute desire it tempted
In the flood of impressions and memories
Effortlessly.

Reading of "Synesis 2"

The speaker confesses about a unique and alluring meeting between her poem and a teardrop of a male recipient. From here, analogical sensitivities are created between the poem and the teardrop of the male recipient. The speaker feels that these analogical sensitivities are stamped in her since birth.

Common in symbolist poetry, the speaker breaks conventions and is not willing to be trapped in the conventions. Like in a conquered city, the male recipient penetrates the rooms of her brain; his silent desire towards the speaker is tempting and answered to him while she is drenched with the flood of impressions and memories, which flow effortlessly. In this *Ars Poetica* poem, the process of writing the poetry includes elements of dictated, guided hallucinated fantasy that are presented by a one-time meeting between the speaker-poet and the male recipient. This is a meeting which includes alluring sensitivities and conquered violence that has sexual meanings (the activity of penetration). The dialogue between these alluring sensitivities and conquered violence creates the poem in its one-time uniqueness.

An Avant Garde Painting

I am swept up in the poem
Spiral among red flowers
As in a great space
Of an avant garde painting.

My dry eyes filled with time lost to me
My poem: a sea

And you hover between the forms of my lips
Your love flickers mysteriously
Wandering with new hope.

And then the water is reflected on the rim of my day

In yellowing light pretending to be sun.

Reading of "Avant Garde Painting"

The poem amalgamates the process of writing the poem with love to the male recipient, a motif that is quite common in the poetry of Edith Covensky. While writing the poem, the speaker feels that she is swept away between the lines of the poem, ascending between the red flowers like in a big space of an avant garde painting. Here comes to fruition the symbolist portrait of the poem: enchanting, mysterious, foggy, indecipherable, and mystic. The dry eyes of the speaker are filled with the time that she is losing in the accumulating flow within her poetry, like a sea. Here, the speaker turns to her beloved, the male recipient. He hovers between the forms of her lips, and his love, until now flickered secretly, is open wide and wanders while it is full of new hope.

The end of the day for the speaker is not to come. In a tone of disappointment and acceptance, she describes the waters that are reflected at the end of the day in a yellow light like the sun. This is an embarrassed pretension because it is not like a plentiful sun—generous—but it is a depressed light, which becomes yellow, like when flowers wither; it is a dwindling, extinguishing light. This way, the poem that starts with a delightful push continues as a poem that grows to the width of the ocean, a stream that quenches the dry eyes of the speaker, despite the time that she is losing. The stream continues with its flickering love in hiding, but it opens towards a new hope, and it arrives to the end while fading and dying.

Therefore, although there are mystic, blocked, and symbolist characteristics of the poem, we can locate in it a plot that moves in a causal path that is beginning with a sweeping push and ends with withering and dying.

A Flower of Drunkenness

I delude myself
Clear-headed calm between fragments of my verse
Mocking out of excitement
At a moment of enchanted love.

I have such desire
Emerging between the words
Crowded in silence.

And the poem is born
A sublime halo entangled within me
Enfolded in pure writing.

And something primal rises from the water
A flower of drunkenness
A kindled ode runs in me
Tumbles on the page.

Reading of "A Flower of Drunkenness"

The process of writing the poetry is spellbinding, hidden, and mystic. The poet deludes herself that she is does not separate herself from the earthly reality while writing poetry. She feels calm and lucid between the fragments of her verses. Also, she feels led astray out of excitement in a moment of magical love. Therefore, even in this poem, the writing of the poetry and the love entwine with each other. The writing of the poetry is a result of a tremendous passion that bursts from the words and is crowded in silence. This is the enchanted moment in which a poem is born, and the halo of light is sublime, sprouts, and is entangled within the speaker.

The same halo of light, celestial and enchanted, is enfolded in the pure writing of the poem. Again, the process of a mystic and enchanted birth is documented. Something primal rises from the water, and indeed, the beginning of life is in the water, in the ancient ocean. The same primal something that rises from the water is an intoxicating flower—a kindled ode running inside the speaker, falling on the page, while she is fertilizing the poem that just blossomed.

Like every symbolist poem, even this poem is not confined to any certain place and not to any national, social, or historical reality. The metaphorical pictures of the poem are complex and produce a dreamy feeling of imaginary fantasy.

Another Poem for Van Gogh

Your hand is stretched out between pages
Of the book folding
In silent trembling
And its sketch is warm
Enchanting in this rendition
The fruit of my pen
My paintbrush.

I have become a poet of fragile things
Interlaced in me in clear precision
Curling on the poem's page
Awakening thought.

And the poetical outburst is splendid
Exalted in freedom
Multi-hued
Encompassing ordered words
Colors rise
One against the other.

Reading of "Another Poem for Van Gogh"

The poem demonstrates an admiration of the colorful paintings of Van Gogh, although this admiration is coming with restraint. The first line of the poem binds the hand of the artist with the pages of the speaker's poetry book. The sketch of the hand of the artist is folded in silent trembling, and it is warm and full of magic. It is like a parent's touch that comes and protects at once. The verse ends with the joining of her pen and the brush of the speaker, a testimony to the influence of the art of Van Gogh's drawing on the art of the poet's writing.

Later on, the speaker documents the process of writing the poetry; she is the poet of fragile things interlaced within her in clear precision. The curling of the page awakens thoughts. The verse that ends the poem documents the process of writing the poetry in a totally opposite way. There are no more fragile things, which are woven in the speaker in clear precision in a way that awakens thoughts, but there are volcanic outbursts of boiling, bubbling lava.

This is a poetic, radiant, sublime, free, and multicolored outburst. It includes organized words and colors, the colors of Van Gogh, which compete with one another in the brightness that they project. The paradoxical, harsh contradiction of two opposite processes of writing poetry—fragile and interweaving versus an outburst like a volcano—give the poem a symbolist, hidden, enchanted, mysterious, and mystic element.

Voices of the Sea

"At the heart of everything rests a great pain,
and it is the river, and we are the banks."
(Dalia Magnet)

The poems rush to me
In words of shadow and memory
Squadrons in the night unfolding on the scene.

And a voice of the sea leaps in the motion
Like a bird on a proper course
Flies to her origin
Journeying on the mountain of God.

Thus is the idea of the poem born in me:
A curled wick of Gold
An exact autumnal sign
Founded within me.

Reading of "Voices of the Sea"

The process of writing the poetry is explained here in reverse, like a movie that is seen from the ending to the beginning. The poems for which the writing is already completed flow towards the speaker-poet in words of shadow and memory. Of course, like the night squadrons that integrate with the view, the poems bring with them the voice of the ocean that is a constant horizontal murmur, like a bird that flies in its course towards its native land. The bird flies in a course that brings her to the mountain of God (refers to Mt. Sinai, on which, according to Jewish tradition, the Torah was given to the children of Israel by Moses).

The last verse of the poem completes the first verse, in the way that it documents the birth of the poem. Here, the symbolist process of writing poetry is expressed: it is hidden; it is magical; it is enchanting; it is mystic, veiled, and ambiguous. A twisted cord of gold and an exact autumnal sign is found within the speaker. In this way, a symbolist poem is born and woven. The flight of the bird to its homeland, to the mountain of God, is like the path of the poem from the moment it was conceived until the moment of its complete realization. The reference to the mountain of God as a desired place one wishes to visit gives the poem its enchanting and mystical portrait.

Love Embraces Love

Love embraces love
Flourishes at the touch
Thaws into life after coldness
Beautiful as the sea

Quiet and virginal.

And after love has survived
The basic creation clings to me
In rhymes new and old
As in a thawed instant of a poem.

And already my tongue tangles in play
As in a new book
All of whose answers are right.

Reading of "Love Embraces Love"

Like many of the poems of Edith Covensky, this poem here is a combination of a love poem and a poem which describes the process of writing the poetry. The love here is so intense and daring that its beauty is comparable to an ocean. Nonetheless, the love is also described as virginal and quiet, the opposite of intense, daring love that is bound with the ocean. Moreover, comparing the love to the water (ocean) brings to mind *Song of Songs*, in which the love is stirring and sweeping one away so much so that "many waters cannot quench love." It is certain that the allusion to the overflowing love in *Song of Songs* gives strength to the description of love. Also, the opening line of the poem, which is also the title of the poem ("Love Embraces Love"), brings to mind the next line of *Song of Songs*: "His left arm is under my head, and his right arm embraces me." Even this allusion to *Song of Songs* reinforces the intensity of the love, which is based on this given poem.

The love in this poem blossoms and grows with the touch of lovers' hands and yields new life after a long period of separation and stagnation. Now the love, after it is thawed, is virginal and quiet. Now the love that survived the near fatal freezing functions like a starting point to writing new and old poems. The thawing of the spirit of creation of the poetry is conditioned and dictated by the thawing of the love.

Consequently, the tongue of the speaker-poet becomes like a whirlwind, entangled in a game of words, which populate the poem like "as in a new book all of whose answers are right." This teaches you that the end of the process of writing poetry is compared to a new book in which all the questions are written and all the answers are valid. The thawing of the love enables the thawing of the poetry, and in these two cases, in the love—like in the poetry—the beginning that is sprouting is promising as well.

I am Addicted to Illusion

I am addicted to illusion
Annul time between the folds of water
My self-amused desire flows
My poem: a feather.

And my eyes are revealed in the clear redness
Defining the day as if I were a painter
My language realizes my love.

And the poem in a sketch like a flower
Living in precious light
Shaking free like a dancing winged bird
In sun absorbing sun.

Reading of "I am Addicted to Illusion"

It is easy to identify the symbolist portrait of the given poem. The atmosphere is mysterious, unclear, imaginary, and hidden. It is impossible to place it in the earthly reality that is either an imaginary dream or a fantasy. To which allusion is the speaker addicted? How does she reject or cancel the time, and what are the folds of water? In what way is her desire amused? What is her desire? To whom is her desire directed?

The sequence of the poem does not provide answers to these questions. Her eyes are exposed to the bright red of the erupting dawn, which is emerging from the darkness of the clouds. Only she defines the day like she is a painter. This is the way her language realizes her love.

An Air

My time is wind
Roaming among words contradicting one another
Glistening in a bustle of a day
And a primeval illusion
And a dark sun floats to the water's edge
And night plays
In blue language exiled from bank to bank
Like a note flowing on the page
Covered by music
With love extended in jest
Growing in the harvest of my dream
Poured out in summer's longing
And a color of gleaming earth
And light enfolded insistent on being a poem.

Reading of "An Air"

Like in the tradition of symbolist poetry, the poem is based on statements, descriptions, and phrases, which are pruned one from another illogically. The poem demonstrates a constant restlessness that expresses itself with movement from one theme to another: a primeval illusion, a dark sun floating on the edge of the water, a night that is playing in blue language exiled from bank to bank, like a note flowing on the page and covered by music, and more.

The poem continues with love extended in jest, growing in a dreamy harvest, poured with longing for the summer, and a color of gleaming earth. Only at the end of the poem, in its last line, do we realize the purpose of the complete poem, and the purpose is writing poetry: "and light enfolded insistent on being a poem."

The poem strikes the reader with a sensual abundance of colors, descriptions, and metaphors, which act on all of the senses of the reader. Consequently, the poem extracts the reader from its earthly and materialistic existence and leads the reader to a mystic, veiled, and imaginary world— a world of delightful and alluring fantasy. There is no doubt that the poem demonstrates an intense loyalty to the tradition of symbolist poetry at its best.

High Waters

I am immersed in the grace of the moment
Among words joining words
In a hidden game
Imagined in the grace of language
And clear stars
And high water flowing in the mixture of time
And the void of a street
And the order of a poem written in confusion
On the state of night
Across the sweep of sand.

Reading of "High Waters"

Like many of the *ars poetica* poems of Edith Covensky, the symbolist frame functions as the beginning point to describe the process in which the poetry is written. The moment of creation is the moment of grace in which words connect to words in a hidden and secret game, and it requires its fabricated portrait in the grace of the language.

The process of creating the poetry brings to mind clear stars, high waters, flowing in a mix of time and the void of the dark street. The organized lines of the poem are written in the tumult of creation; at the end of the creation, the poem is engraved on the state of the night, across the sweep of the sand. Therefore, like in the symbolist poetry, the process of writing the poem is gloomy, veiled, hidden, and mystic, and only these outstanding people are able to enter the enchanting atmosphere of writing poetry.

Anachronism

I alienate myself from time
In an abundance of words heaped on the shelf of night
Like in the matter hidden in the poem
In the flicker of a dream
And the meld of language formulated in words of love
Inventing the size of the sky.

And the day blues
Turns to sand pressed to water
Caught in great motion
Flowing among the subjects of the wind
And living passion
And an archaic memory emptied in me
Drifting light on the page.

Reading of "Anachronism"

(Another ars poetica poem by Edith Covensky, which is designed as a product of a symbolist poem.)

While she is writing her poetry, the speaker-poet alienates herself from the passing time while an abundance of words are accumulating and piling onto the shelf of night. In the poem, there is hidden raw material, like the flickering of a dream and like the chaos of the words of the language. This leads her to express herself in a framework of love while she is formulating words the size of the sky. In a mysterious, imaginary, mystic way, a broad spectrum of feelings is created while she is writing the poem: the day blues; the sand pressed to water flows among the subjects of the wind; and the living passion and archaic memory are emptied inside the speaker and drifts easily on the page. The writing of the poetry is compared, therefore, to a surging flood of feelings and associations that carry one away. These feelings are developed and contradicted in the fertile, amazing imagination of the speaker-poet.

I Rise in the Midst of a Black Sea

I rise in the midst of a black sea
In a poem preserved in the catalogue of the night
In a fragile moment invading me
Across the noise of the rain
And a tumult of wind curling amid all the arches.

And then I touch the sky
Strict with words tumbling in a dream
Like divine speech turning in me
In a version of pain
And the becoming of time
And a memory still in the street.

Reading of "I Rise in the Midst of a Black Sea"

The poem demonstrates a Gothic, dark, and gloomy atmosphere: The speaker rises in the middle of a black sea. The catalogue of the night invades the speaker's body in a fragile moment where she is defenseless, and the noise of the pouring rain and the tumult of the wind curling amid all the curves are heard. Nonetheless, despite the Gothic darkness, there is no surrendering: The speaker rises up; she stays upright despite the black sea's rage. So therefore, despite the atmosphere, which imposes horror, the speaker does not give up or withdraw. Furthermore, she ascends upward and touches the sky to teach you; not only does the speaker not give up, but she is also full of pride. Like in a mystic seance, like in an isolated experience that is cut off from the earthly reality, the words of the poem are rolled up in a dream, like a divine speech churning inside the speaker.

Indeed, the entire mystic process of creating a poem is not devoid of pain, is not devoid of sorrow or grief. After its peak (like when the speaker rises above in the middle of the black sea) comes the moment of fading and despondency: after not so long, everything that remains will be only a silent memory. In this typical symbolist poem, the writing of the poetry is documented as a mystic, hidden, and veiled experience that has darkness and pain, pride, and a gush of penetrating creation.

A Legend

"Sir: It is time. The summer has grown exceedingly large."
(Rainer Maria Rilke)

My lips are grace
Pleasure revealed in memory's light
In the form of a poem
Accumulates in a kind of legend
Reconciled under the cover of dark
Flowing in the confusion of time
In an ancient plot
Opposite dim eyes
And illusions completing one another.

And I sing alone
Touching the night
Roaming in the fusion of invention
In a game revealing my charms
And in love diluted in the wind
And in rain bursting sweetly like a tear falling on the page.

Reading of "A Legend"

The symbolism in the poem demonstrates hallucinatory fantasy that is absorbed with secrecy and mystic, gloomy, veiled mystery, which is hard to decipher. The speaker's lips in the poem are like grace, like pleasure, which is revealed in the memory of the light. The same pleasure, which comes from the grace of the speaker's lips, is anchored in the structure of the poem, unified in the framework of a legend. This legend feels comfortable in the dark, reconciled under the cover of the dark. The same legend that has its origin in the grace of the speaker's lips, in the pleasure which is revealed in the memory's light, is clearing the path for the world and making its way. It flows in the maze of dark tunnels, in the confusion of time, which is running out.

In all that, like in an ancient Gothic legend, dim eyes are watching it. With them, hallucinations are flowing and complete each other. The loneliness of the speaker is emphasized in the nightly atmosphere that covers it, while it circles around and merges with the lie. All that is happening like in a game that reveals the charms of the speaker, and her love, which is diluted in the wind, like rain bursting sweetly like a tear falling on the page on which the poem is written. Even here, the atmosphere is diluted with secrecy and mystery. Nonetheless, it merges with another level of gentle, captivating sensuality. Even here, the process of writing the poem is merged with the symbolism, which is the foundation of the poem.

A Type of Speech

"Man is born with some kind of sadness."
(S. Yizhar)

I am prone to a type of speech
Gleaming
Colorful
Like the language of lust
And a hidden uproar
Echoing in a circular riddle
Emptied from the night.

And I exult in poem
In compact writing
Metaphoric
Appended to loneliness in a draft turning in me.

I become a nihilist
Appealing all the words
In a moment of stillness
And pure dialogue
And the murmur of music
Guessing something of this time.

Reading of "A Type of Speech"

The speaker confesses her attraction to this type of speech, which is radiant and colorful like the language of lust. The same type of speech sounds like a hidden moan, maybe the moaning of the sea. The speeches echo in mysterious circles that are empty from the maze of the night. At the same time, the speaker is full of cheerfulness, which overflows. She is rejoicing at the poem in her compact, metaphoric writing, and it attaches to the loneliness that is hidden within her.

In this manner, the first verse, which opens with a full, overflowing rejoicing, is completed and signed with a draft that is wrapped in loneliness. In this way, the speaker becomes a nihilist: she lost her faith in words; she lost her faith in earthly reality, which is supposed to be firm. Nonetheless, in a moment of stillness, the speaker still feels closeness to the pure conversation and to the whisper of the music. Only in this way, she can guess something of this time: a time where her faith in words is exhausted, but nevertheless, the connection to the pure dialogue and to the murmur of music is not lost. The poem is based on the writing of poetry, which is full of contradictions that are difficult to bridge, which is acceptable in symbolist poetry.

ANTHOLOGY:
SELECTED SYMBOLIST POEMS
BY EDITH COVENSKY

Only God Sees Me

I write in the dispute of night
Separate from the wind
Circling in a lucid poem
Fearful of becoming a sun.

And I mark heavens
In a drawing of a dream
And liquid waters
And the yellowest sand.

Only God sees me
Among options of imagined words
Bound in this speech
Tumbling to the luminous place.

A Tribute to a Poem

"I was told there is a way to land where the sun sets."
(Dalia Rabikowich)

I am free
In a biographical version
And a myth resolving amid the possibilities of night
Storing love engendering all my visions.

And I am confused in memory
Freezing time in a day dipped in me
Like a wind bending on the page
In a field of light clasped on tranquil earth.

And my words crowd within me
Enchanted on my lips
Flowing opposite the wheel of the sun
In a most sensual poem.

I Am Born From the Dark

I am born from the dark
Daughter of laughter
Trapped in a vision
Circling at the water's edge
Flowing in a place that never was

And I draw another sun
Set in the roar of time
Melding in the tension of wind
With quick writing
And the trembling of dream.

And then I am left in the strength of the poem
Clear like the flash of lightning
Digging into me
A voice of a bird
Confused in crooked rain
Opposite torn eyes rising from the sea.

Psychosis

I am near the folio of time
Curling in the rhythm of day
Flowing across the sound of water.

And still I join words
As in a parody of night embroidering my fear
Breaking in a fragment of gloom.

And you take a fistful of my love
In silence spread like in an open field
To teach me word after word

And then the poem becomes a presence
In pure thought crowding within me
Thriving in a summer's day doubling my pain.

Dirge

I awaken at first rain
Almost mythic
Curl up in a childish plot
Tucked away in the landscape's pall.

And then I burn night
Nihilistic bursting time
Give myself up to the wind
Diluted in a moment of grace.

And my day is periodic
A kind of metaphor tattooed into all that exists
Like mute basalt
And a dirge of sea
And a poem of God.

Identities

I annul time
Standing across the night
In a cluster of enchanting love
Rolling in a girl's chat pointing to the whole sky.

My day is still
Flows with my longings in a childish plot
Curling on the sand
Moving from identity.

And I sing with the wind
Circle the length and breadth
Between adorning stars
Drawn in blue pencil.

A Blue Bird

My illusion becomes
Cropped from blue power of the night
Like a fancy drawing up stars.

And love cleaves to me
Glinting in the give of time
Touching me like a flower
And warm sand
A softest earth.

And the poem plays in a strange moment
Like a marginal pause
And the longing of a blue bird circling on water.

An Illusory Day

My day is illusory
Restores love perfected in me
Saved in the archives in which I focus all the sun.

And I walk solitary
A silhouette among the landscape shards
Nourishing the poem.

And still I scatter my fear with fluent rhythm
And exact rhyme
Created from water.

I Act Between the Tricks of the Night

"The sea made a sound and
in the midst of the sound—silence."
(S. Y. Agnon)

I act between the tricks of the night
Eccentric in the cycle of such time
Bound in words phrased in me
Perfecting with fiction roaming on the page
Clear with thought at the glorious moment.

And I become an optimistic woman
Gathering stars flickering near the dark
Murmuring roaring across the sea
Flowing like a living love
Blending with the fire of God.

And then all leads to the poem
Focusing on the relish of composition
In yearning silent in the street
Blushing, everlasting, curling in a whisper
Moving under the highest sun.

Monologue

"The story, so I calm myself, refuses to be an illusion."
(Meir Shalev)

I found love that is not consumed
Precise clear
Near-far
Gathered together
Joined at the hand of the poet
Creating sun
And a slight wind
And a flowering memory
As in a dizzying poem
And a monologue of day
Among scattered things
Clarified in such a night
Joining to all words.

Longing

My mother is still
Hovering at a height of star chasing star
Absorbing all the words.

And the wind plays
Flows among the stains of the day
With intoxicated longing circling above the water.

And she crosses the sea
With yearning catching a ridge
And with a voice echoing in me
Whispering night.

For Wassily Kandinsky

Love rules me
Conquers silently
Wraps my womb
Across windings of a road
And a hot sun
Among rhymes turning with the advent of spring
And units of first words
And flowers in a mosaic of a dream
And cracked thought
Breaking among the shards of the night
A grayish rain
And the beat of transparent longing
In the color of the dark.

Self-Portrait

My simple language connects to the night
Twirls in the street
Across stone
And iron
And signs of people
And speech like wind
And disruptions of shade
And cracked words
Among materials joining within me
Like citations of a day
And a marginal biography
Wilting in this metaphor
Turning to a point fused onto the page.

Impression

My day's current rises
Soaked in earth-colors
And my laughter wilts
My face is chaste
My utterance simple at sunset.

And from the stream of my autobiographical poem
Made impure as if useless
Rises my experimental voice

Like the voice of the water bird.

We are two people who love
(you say)
Not revolutionaries
Fragile products
In winter's white
And low sun.

Monograph

I found a hint of joy in you
And positive energies
And even dedicated to you
A monograph of love.

You hesitated for a while
Stayed in the kingdom of your poems
Influencing in the night
The next verse.

The order of words was not accidental
My diary was clinical
With no signs of childishness

And you did not notice the woman in love:
The operator at play.

I am Creating a Flower

I am creating a flower
And a woman and man
Descendants of sun

And I fold a medium fig leaf
And a petal
In the fingertips of my love.

And a tree reaches the wall of the house
In the zone of my childhood
Masize
Pierced in ancient Braille.

And I write words on scraps of paper
And on the edges of last sidewalks
And on hands that catch in
The brittle air

And my content
Mingles with Bartok's Dance Suite
1923.

I Became a Modern Painter

I turn the day into fiction
Between the clippings of the poem
In which may easily be read such things
As light shadow and sea.

I became a modern painter
Crossing the borders of time
With summer emotions

And with amusing warmth
And almost walking rain.

A Possibility for Poetry

I feel some elevation of spirit
Charmed by the possibility of poetry
In the dim high night
Try to seize the time
And the tempo of your breath

From my point of view
This a day's attempt
And embodiment of your being
A first breakthrough
Appeasing even God.

My Mother Perceived as Fiction

My mother perceived as fiction
Her walk fetching
Her body composed of my pranks

She is energetic and daring
Her windings staying beyond reality.

Her place is sublime
The wrinkles on her face separated and combine
Her dress is blue
Her motion: a flower
Enclosing all summer.

I Also Have the Temper of Poets

I also have the temper of poets
The burden of my legacy in its realistic measure
Arouses some important love.

And perhaps I have no true rendition of this poem
My love is plaited in my mouth
Twined in my breast
On ordinary days.

As far as I am concerned
This is a dated biography
Crumbs of thought
A poem anticipated
Justifying its own existence.

Stardust

I was born in an instant
A very small piece of time
Flowing between the words
In a poem not yet written
And in a place which night had not reached.

And this like a tale that entrances me
(in my terms)
Eager
Light
Sprinkling on me a little dust from the stars

There is something childish in me
That leads me lighthearted through the days
Free to squander

And all that preserves me perhaps
Is the inability to die
In the fire dissolved in me
When I seal the poem.

Summary of a Poem

"It is good for me this way;
the reckoning is almost obvious."
(Gabriel Preil)

My verses are enveloped in silence
Flowing among many illusions
Restless
Seeking a little for me
A summarizing poem
By all accounts

And in a scattered instance
Love comes to me
Rocking in the cradle
Rolling on the grass.

My soft words are befogged
Anxiety is here
Focused freely on the poem
Buried in confusion.

To Plato

Your love astounds
Open to the night
A kind of declared musing on a national page
Flooding the landscape.

And my speech is naked to the edge of confusion
Analytical at the tip of the paintbrush
Tempting between the lines
Revolving in platonic awkwardness
Uplifting my soul.

What love courses through me
Its speech frugal
Its edge slippery
Bound in the poem.

The Silence Insulates Me

"We are awakened by the same sun."
(Limor Naschmias)

I acquire your love
A live flower warming in the sun
Fragile between dream and dream
Dilute among syllables of the night.

Here starts the clarification
Adorning itself
Exposed to the poem
Looking at me with sad eyes
A faint smile on my lips.

And the memory is within my reach
Your shadow curls on the wall
Revolves in creation signifies

The silence insulates me.

Metaphysics

I compose words
Like a storm at the edge of the table
Scattered enveloping day
Revolving in sheaves of light.

It is love alone which time gives me
To bring it into the secret of my creation
To emerge from its yearnings
In careful rejoicing

The vision is delicate:
A gifted novice of poetry is behind the words
Sprout of my thought
An axis on which I turn.

Still Life

You feel my loneliness
As an allegory of my human existence
But this is not reason enough to freeze the day.

I speak from my dream
Hiding behind the obsession
Surrendering to your glance.

My small world is great
Also laden with stars
And a completely open view
And a scent of color in a silent painting.

Oriental Lamentation

My dream is drawn in free rhythm
Mixed with alchemy
Whirling among streets of sand
Clothed in sad beauty.

The music is desire and sadness
Floating like oriental lamentation
Among rare flowers.

What feeling appeases me
My laughter is drunken
My body wanders exiled

This is possible only thanks to the wind.

I Am Silent as a Flower

My love is hot in the midst of illusion
Lifts off in splendor among lucid memories
Washing over my window.

And children play among flowers
Entwined within the loneliness
Blushing at sunset
Shaking themselves off at dawn.

I am silent as a flower
Created in light engulfing me
Glowing in my path
Roaring with a smile
Falling silent.

A Net of Words

I stride along my one-way street
Operating in such peace
Whispering my secrets

And my voice is soft in the bolt of cloth
Swept away in a net of words
At the end of the same day.

It is easy for me to invent your love
Before time obscures me
Confused by such intensity
Set in silence.

Now a chilling wind blows
Desolate into my palms
Clear as a poem.

I Become a Dreamer of Jerusalem

I become a dreamer of Jerusalem
Traversing time
In colorful illusion
Plunging in my depths
Between chapters of a paradoxical day.

The rocking is human on three pages
Gripping the base of the wall
The freedom limiting my scope.

And my poem is a secret
My survival a puzzle knotted with exaltation of soul
And shattered longings.

Wall

God speaks to me
Among quick words
Warming a day of scattered rain
Falling opposite words whispering love
Exactly as in a round night
Close to premial pain
Written on the wall
Descending in yellow time.

Why have I all these thoughts
Facing a bus ascending the street
Rolling a poem on dark asphalt
Among words enfolding
To a lovely language of the moment
Like an ancient dirge
A silent shadow turning among domes and arches
And crowded people
And stone.

A Poem in Prose

My poem is a draft
Delicately charming to the point of pain
A stain of color on parched soil
A living plot among ruins.

Great love arises from the words
Moving signs
Opening points of spring
Are hidden in them.

And my day is silent
Passing from word to word
Free in combination.

How I erupt blending in the poem
My wanderings long in the sunset.

Testimony

"I am a collection of many autumns."
(Gabriel Preil)

My eyes quiver drunkenly
Bear my loneliness like a scarlet bird
Silent among the droplets of darkness.

My time is entwined in the poem
Like the testimony of the poet
And as a silent promise
Spinning magic.

I am a woman of dreams:
My light is shadow
A fictitious sun embroiders my words
Scented in flight
Open to love.

YAIR MAZOR

I Sit in an Icy Landscape

I sit in an icy landscape
Unwooded and torn
River and hard

And Jerusalem opens
Her powers before me
Concealed in a womb of stones
Concealed in courses of stones
Like courses of words in lines
Words.

In the night I remove them
One by one
Two by two
And discover a grand Byzantine stone
And Byzantine sand
And wood.

Geological Sand

I am a desert rover
Confused amidst fire burned substances
And geological sand
And savage bird sounds

Play on a hot yellow ground
And my eyes blaze amidst the shadows
Whispering conciliatory words
With a roar gleaming in me
Spread out like in an open field

The night covers my body
Rotating in childishly covered silence
Rolling in a main street

There I wander naked among the seashells.

I Paint a Sun

I paint a sun
A fantasy in the spirit of time
A deafening illusion I have no escape from
Coupled with me
Charisma strengthening in my memory
Hallucinating dabbling in magic.

There is actually here the very making of the poem
A woman seeking love on a mad day
Crouching between the lines
With limpid desire
Like a flower in the abundance of light.

Songbird

I draw words and symbols on the earth
Stamped in my language
They engulf me
Rolling in laughter and sobs.

I become a songbird
Rejoicing in my young voice
Quivering in the tumult with a clown's smile

And love grows dizzying
Echoing within me
The impulse whispers within.

Words Binding Words

"The words did their work alone
flying through the air like birds on fire."
(Aharon Appelfeld)

My puzzle poem is clarified in festivity
Drawn to the sun in concentrated intensity
Gusty in deception
Nobly mobilized in tune.

And I am like a shore bird
Gliding in this optimism
Grayish aware of the light
Shaking free in my flight.

And the words bind words
In an enthusiastic scheme revealing my poem
Devised in me in summer.

Nostalgia

I have strong nostalgia in my head
Laden with memories greater than I
For I see them now
Like heroes from history
In narrow striped clothing
As if from the war.

There is no place under the sun
Where you will not see such men
Sometimes as large as Goya's giant.

Perhaps in these stars they seem
Each man in his fashion
Late in this night.

The Ocean Shore

I sit in a corner by the ocean shore
Arranging alone an account of my day
My words are tortuously fragile

Perhaps my love is also imaginary

I grasp almost no real memory
Playing childishly with paradoxes
Indicating a poem
And fiery stars
And words without uses

And the erotic transpires in my body
Generates knowledge
And the stuff of the poem
Torn from words not in the dictionary.

For Baudelaire

I am at your side in the whirlwind
Rolling about the wandering Canaanite
And my spirit is a bird whispering a poem
Playing music in a wide night

And my low hovering in the vicissitudes of day
Maddened by daydreams
Losing my senses

And I am flowing sand caressing your body
Frightened childishly by the tune.

What is the enigma of longing
The shadow of fear in mutation
Baudelaire's curse in the rain.

The sea is my expanse between the piers
My choir is night.

My Lips are a Flower

I was created from the ethereal material of the poem
Rolling in the text
Revolutionary in desire
And my eye investigates at the slope of the street
Painting my dreams.

My yearning is delicate in the dark
My words are clarified at an abyss edge
Silent in waiting

My lips are a flower.

And then I return to the basics:
Light flows between exchanged words
First fire beguiles
Water to my dusty words.

In the end I am a wind blowing between the words
My sketches are quick
My love exactingly decorated.

Lucid Writing

I hoard words
In a big book
Slippery
Turning into night
Adorning the time
Abounding with beauty
And stars
Like a lofty sketch
And a new autobiography according to all the definitions
And an eternal composition
Enchanting in an attempt at lucid writing
In rounded handwriting
Becoming with the speed of sound
In a playful poem
And with memory breaking in the noise of day
And hard earth
Across a blue sea
Flowing in a chain of things
Like revealed language
And tune playing with tune
True
Invented.

Confession

My mother yearns for the sun
Ascends drenched in light
Perfumed in delusion.

Her puzzling being confuses with imagination
Connecting me to the poems.

She is my great deliverance
Exulting among the words
In sophisticated rhymes from pole to pole
Whispering in trance.

And I flow in this excitement
Whirl dazedly
Melted into the sunset
Poured out to the stars.

I am an Anonymous Poet

I am an anonymous poet
Coming from the absurdity between light and darkness
Seeping into a fictitious poem
With a love rising from my dream.

And my day churns in me rustling
Flutters within me
In a disorder of voices
Magically holding me.

My joy is mischievous because of the toils.

And suddenly I have the urge to love
With transparent words
Stopping time
In a quick sentimental instant.

Black Flowers

My mother lives at the edge of day
And old time
Rolling between streams of words
And black flowers.

I have no haven from memory
Pulling speech with a dark tongue
Crouching in the tumult of night
And blood revealed like water.

And I burn stars concealed in the dark
In a confused order
Between the evil impulse
And the good
In a composite of things
Like the tune of a murky water
Sneaking into a place like this.

An Apocalyptic Wind

"I am the wind that blows
and dies out in dark water."
(Czeslaw Milozs)

I circle as fast as the wind
And my broad shadow hovers
Breaking forth against the curves of my body

Amidst the little light remaining.

And a tree grows on half of the world
And idiotic minimalist
Upsetting my balance

And what is hard in me is left hanging
And the light is yellow like the crust of the earth.

Last words I heard were my vow of silence
In a scenery of sea
Rocking from star to star.

YAIR MAZOR

A Yellow Stain

"As I stood between the living and the dying."
(Saul Tchernichovsky)

My poem is preserved
Turning with the suppleness of day
In a stain of yellow light
Steeped in the sun.

I have an obligation to the night
Like a black presence
Symbolic
Thought wholly a sinner.

From childhood I absorb all I see around me
In a strange landscape
And carnival air
Blowing in gaping darkness
And in the noise of high waters.

I Invent the Sun

I am caught up in the signs of the day
Enchanted seduced in the flow
Between objects and symbols
Smudging the rules of the poem.

I hoard the breadth of words
Invent the sun
As if grasping the celestial bodies
Hovering above all this.

Ever since I pierce my sadness across an
Archetypical sea
Gnawing away in the sand
Construct my poems daily
To conquer the dark.

ABOUT THE AUTHOR

Dr. Yair Mazor is Professor Emeritus of modern Hebrew and Biblical literature at the University of Wisconsin–Milwaukee. To date, Professor Mazor has authored 30 scholarly books and more than 250 articles and critical essays that have been published in the USA, Israel, and numerous European countries. Dr. Mazor is a popular guest lecturer and has spoken to audiences throughout Europe and many other venues around the world.

Among the many scholarly awards Dr. Mazor has received are the Sadan Prize and the Shpan Prize for two of his books, the Baron Prize for Excellency in the field of Jewish studies, the distinguished teaching award by the University of Wisconsin–Milwaukee, and the Friedman Prize, a national award for the most distinguished Hebrew literature scholar in the United States.

In his military service, Dr. Mazor acted as a combat paratrooper, as well as an instructor of parachuting.

www.ingramcontent.com/pod-product-compliance
Lightning Source LLC
Chambersburg PA
CBHW072046090426
42733CB00032B/2290